Etsy

The Complete Beginners Guide to Growing a Successful Etsy Business in 30 Minutes or Less!

Copyright © 2015

All rights reserved. No part of this book may be reproduced in any form without permission in writing from the author. Reviewers may quote brief passages in reviews.

Disclaimer

No part of this publication may be reproduced or transmitted in any form or by any means, mechanical or electronic, including photocopying or recording, or by any information storage and retrieval system, or transmitted by email without permission in writing from the publisher.

While all attempts and efforts have been made to verify the information held within this publication, neither the author nor the publisher assumes any responsibility for errors, omissions, or opposing interpretations of the content herein.

This book is for entertainment purposes only. The views expressed are those of the author alone, and should not be taken as expert instruction or commands. The reader of this book is responsible for his or her own actions when it comes to reading the book.

Adherence to all applicable laws and regulations, including international, federal, state, and local governing professional licensing, business practices, advertising, and all other aspects of doing business in the US, Canada, or any other jurisdiction is the sole responsibility of the purchaser or reader.

Neither the author nor the publisher assumes any responsibility or liability whatsoever on the behalf of the purchaser or reader of these materials.

Any received slight of any individual or organization is purely unintentional.

Table of Contents

Introduction

Chapter 1 - Have you heard About Etsy?

Chapter 2- Important Matters to Know

Chapter 3- You Gotta Be Choosy

Chapter 4- Organizing and Setting-Up

Chapter 5- Photography Musts

Chapter 6 -More Tips that Successful Sellers Know

Conclusion

Introduction

First and foremost I want to thank you for downloading the book, "Etsy Selling- *The Complete Beginners Guide to Growing a Successful Etsy Business in 30 Minutes or Less!*.

In this book you will learn how to start your own online shop and make it big in Etsy. Consider this books as your quick-start guide with all the important things, tips, advice and techniques you must consider to get you Etsy shop in top shape.

Etsy had various features and tools which might overwhelm newbie like you hence, we will introduce to you those features and how you can actually use them in setting-up your shop.

Moreover we will teach you how to keep your items on top of the search list and what to do to attract buyers and encourage repeat orders. Avoid confusion and disappointments when you are not making sales by following the tips from successful sellers on Etsy.

Thanks again for downloading this book, I hope you enjoy it!

Chapter 1

Have you heard About Etsy?

The internet is flourished with various websites and it's safe to say that online shops or online markets are prevalent as well. Ebay, Amazon and Etsy are the most popular online markets nowadays. However, Etsy is focused more on a person's ability to establish their own online shop. They also aim to empower individuals to take part in economic growth. But compared with Ebay, Etsy has a smaller coverage in terms of items. Among the three main categories on Etsy are materials and supplies to create handmade items, handmade items ready for selling and vintage stuffs.

Etsy's Awesome Features

Etsy has various features which make it more appealing to online sellers and consumers.

Social networking - one of the coolest features of Etsy is that you can create your circles, join other teams and groups with the same interests or same items to sell. You can also follow friends with common interests and share finds.

Activity feed - in here you can view the happenings related to you and your friends as well as their "favorites". You can also see who "favorite" your selling items or when it is already sold. Similarly you can see items that were placed in treasury which is another feature on Etsy.

Treasuries - a cool feature where you can create a group according to themes of items that you want to share within the community or simply, the items you like. It is fun and enjoyable since people can leave their comments on your treasure idea. You can also search for other treasuries to gather ideas such as fashion, house decorations or do-itoyourself parties.

Coupon codes - here you can create coupon codes to attract more customers such as percentages off and free shipping. It is a good way to market your shop and gain following. You have the option to turn on or off the coupon codes as well and Etsy will save them for your future use. Likewise you can permanently delete the coupon codes to make sure that they won't be longer in used.

Blogs - another edge of Etsy is that they enable blogging feature which definitely works fine especially for artistic sellers and consumers. The blogs are very specific and relevant in terms of Etsy selling and item purchasing.

Recent items - this is where customers can find items by viewing the constant updates on the recently listed items. Etsy shops can post multiple times in a day to get their items included in the recent items so they can drive more traffic.

Inexpensive - another reason Etsy is popular is because they post and sell items at a very affordable price. Hence more sellers are attracted since they can post items without spending huge amount.

Why More Sellers Choose Etsy

Despite its big competitor, the Ebay, Etsy has become more popular over time for sellers due to the following reasons;

Cost - as we discussed earlier, Etsy is way too cheaper compared to Ebay and other online markets. It charges $0.20 insertion fee and only charges 3.5% selling fee based on the total cost of your items exclusive of the mailing cost.

Clear and working layout - the layout is regularly updated and offers a clean selling approach to customers. The navigation bars are also user-friendly and helpful features are included. The consistency on their layout thumbnail makes it easier for both sellers and buyers to navigate through the website.

Provides specialties - when you already saw the Etsy website, you can actually say that they offer a boutique-like feeling. There are specialties and rare finds such as vintage items that you can easily view.

Longevity of items posting - good thing about Etsy is that they are allowing users to post their items for a month so you don't have to fear of losing your items a week after you posted it.

Starting your online shop with the help of Etsy could be overwhelming especially if you are a traditional merchant or seller.

There is so much for you to learn about Etsy and to master all its features. Don't fret as "professional" Etsy sellers are still learning like you.

There are various things you have to consider before putting up your shop such as your time to allot on each items, the availability of your products and labor charge. All these and more will be discovered as we progress. Let us discussed more of Etsy's advantages and how newbies like you can utilize their system to sell more and earn more!

Chapter 2

Important Matters to Know

Before you actually set-up an account with Etsy and post your items for selling, there are various things you must consider first to ensure your success. As a shop owner, ask yourself if selling your items on Etsy would work for you and your business. Remember that one method which other people applied in their business might not work for you. To re-evaluate your decision, ask yourself of the following essential questions.

Conduct a research - whether you already have a physical shop and items to sell or you are still in the process of choosing which products to sell, doing your research is an important step in joining the E-commerce business. Not just because you have your products listed on Etsy does it mean a sure sale for you. Without planning and strategy, the shop won't be successful regardless of the online market you will enter. Use the internet to gain more facts, information and tips about Etsy. Along the way try to answer the following questions;

- Is there a demand or an audience for your products or items?
- Are there similar items to yours that is being on-sale?
- Who are your competitors with the same products on Etsy?
- Are they making any profits now?
- Would your items be helpful or will meet an individual's needs? What are those needs it can meet?
- Are the customers will be able to imagine the use of your products or items by just staring at a picture or reading its description?
- Do you really know your products? How much it costs in other shops and sellers? Do you think buyers will spend their money for it?

By answering the questions above, you will also be able to find out if selling on Etsy is doable and workable for you.

Originality and uniqueness - another important thing is for you to come up with an original style or design for your items. You see there are hundreds of online sellers out there and some of them perhaps are selling the same items that you also offer. You must differentiate your products from the rest with a fresh concept or feature.

Ask yourself; what are the specific factors that will make your items stand out? After conducting your research you already know now that you do have a competition. Hence, you should find out how to make you items more appealing to the customers over your competitor's.

If the competitor has something to offer that you don't have, think of how to be at par with them. Can you provide quick turnaround? Do you offer affordable prices? After conducting a sufficient amount of research and you have an understanding of your items, think of the specific audience for your products.

Know your market - every type of business has someone to cater to. Determine the type of market that you think will buy and promote your items. Let's say you are selling crafty stuffs, wall decors and the likes, most probably mothers, home decorators and crafts persons will be your customers.

Identifying your market is crucial as this will determine your business' direction and your future expansions if ever. Find out your market's age, sex, interests and occupation and why would they buy your items. Does you market use social media? Can they find you on Etsy? Likewise you must determine if your item is something that would make a repeat sale.

Time to spend- like any other business, one has to allot adequate time with their online shops. Same with a physical shop, your online market also requires maintenance or you will not be successful. Thus, regardless of the sales, you have to regularly look after your shop and track your sales progress on Etsy.

Maintenance of your Etsy shop includes your time and effort and making quality images that would showcase your items to sell. The announcements and promos must be up to date and the instructions are clear and informative. Likewise item descriptions must also use key tag words for easy listings and finds.

Another key to successful Etsy shop is by creating attractive banners and informative shop descriptions. If you will notice, successful sellers on Etsy have specific policies, about page and shipping guidelines which most consumers love. Hence you have to take time in creating these pages for your shop. There are helpful hints you can apply moreover, you can ask another sellers about their opinions since they know what works in Etsy.

Once everything is settled with the shop you created, it doesn't there. The *actual running of your shop* will be next. These include regularly checking the shop, answering customer's issues, queries and comments, updating your listings, replying to sales and checking the status of your shop to see if you are driving adequate traffic.

The feedback that you will get can help you determine what items are popular and salable in your shop. Likewise you can come up with self-evaluation. You can find out the current demand on the market and if you are making sales from it.

Time to Conclude

Finally, you entire shop must possess the "Etsy-style". This is what most consumers are after too. Get familiarize with Etsy's features and functions so you could get the look and feel of an Etsy shop. Nonetheless, it is handmade marketplace which exhibits vibe and style that attracts both sellers and customers.

After re-evaluating your goals and your items, it will be easy for you to decide if Etsy is the perfect marketplace for you and your shop. Once decided, make sure to continue learning the work-around in Etsy, to learn more from its community and to acquire the benefits that Etsy has to offer. This would mean hard work but as long as you love what you are doing, becoming an Etsy seller could be one fulfilling decisions you have ever made.

Chapter 3

You Gotta Be Choosy

And because online shops and online businesses has become the trend, one must carefully weigh her options in setting up an online shop and become an Etsy seller. Aside from product competition, there are a lot more areas to take into consideration for your business to become successful. Thus here are helpful hints before you begin selling.

Choosing the Right Name (Username)

Newbies usually get excited with other stuffs such as ordering supplies and items, item descriptions, possible promos for opening and so on. However many neglected the importance of having a unique username. You can no longer change your name on Etsy not even when you are opening your own shop.

Hence, choosing your name is very essential as this will stick with you and your shop forever.

If possible, try to come-up with a username which is similar to the name of your shop or something relevant to it.

Choosing the Shop's Name

Your shop's name is essential in gaining traffic and that means profit! Consider these when deciding about the name of your shop;

- KISS principleapparently – ,a short and simple name yet unique one can ring a bell when customers are looking for items. Find a name that has recall and avoid longer names.

- Relevance – it is also advisable to have a name with relevance to the items or products you are selling so customers can easily remember.

- Uniqueness – the more original name, the better.

- Readability and searchable – correct spelling and not limiting your shop's name using numbers are helpful. Likewise capitalizing the first letter of each word helps. It will make your shop name searchable and relevant. Associate the shop's name with your products to make it search friendly.

Choose your banner and avatar

Choose a banner that is professionally looking and makes shoppers become more interested to see more. You can also use awesome item photos in your banner to attract customers and they'll get a view of what your shop offers. However if you are not really artsy and does not have the time to create a beautiful banner, there are Etsy sellers that can do provide it for you.

For the avatar, an awesome item photo could also serve as one. It could advertise your shop while communicating within the community.

Choose Your Branding

There is a profusion of designers and sellers on Etsy thus; developing graphic kits with similar looks is an advantage. Make sure your custom listing. Avatar, banner and business cards all have similar image and feel on it.

Choose Your Photos

We will discuss this on a separate chapter but it is also included here since you have to be extra careful and choosy as well in posting images of your items. Etsy, like other online market is an image-driven site and customers usually based their buying decisions on the photos posted. Come up with clutter-free and clear images. Use similar backgrounds as well and practice proper lighting.

Choosing the Price

Apparently, one of the hardest tasks in any kind of business is deciding on a product's price. As you explore, you tend to adjust the prices and learn more on their needs and wants. When setting the price, keep these things in mind;

- Check the competitor's prices and see if they are able to make a sale. You can also see the frequency of their sales. Search other sites to gather and compare the general pricing of the same item.

- Determine the period of time needed to fully accomplish an item. Have a good estimate from the starting point including the hourly wage and supply costs. However be realistic in setting up your hourly wage and better to base on your skills.

Avoid setting too low prices like what newbies tend to do. Remember that most customers rely on the item's quality based on its prices. Your price should reflect quality, time and skills you allot to finish the entire product.

Consider all the others costs and fees for materials, selling, in creating your listings and time spent on communicating with customers. You can also use pricing equations. Likewise, pricing can also be intimidating for starters however, you can break it with existing formulas.

Choose your Products

Perhaps you are reading other articles about Etsy, you should know by now that it has 3 large categories which are the buying and selling of crafts, vintage products and craft supplies. Thus your item should fall into one of these categories. Moreover, your products should be something you actually enjoy doing, it is different and can stand out among the crowd, and the time you need to spend for creating or getting the product.

What to sell

There are a myriad of awesome items that could be found on Etsy thus most newbies are wondering how their items could make an impact to potential buyers.

- If there are items with several sellers such as hair clips and headbands, try making your own style and use unique materials to stand out. Moreover a great photo can make your product stand-out so it should be aesthetically pleasing.
- An undeserved niche could help you establish yourself. Find inspirations in categories and sub-categories and determine where you can make a mark.
- Or better yet, create a new item or re-purpose and recreate existing items. Reinventing things will take some time but these new finds can make you famous and unique in Etsy.

If your products are one of a kind and are something that consumers need and want, you can generate a huge profit as you don't need to compete with competitors with lower prices. However you may need some time to gain trust and loyalty with customers.

Find Your Interest

Etsy offers a unique platform where aspiring online sellers and those who would want to take their shops in the next level can start and succeed. As you spend time, resources and efforts with this new venture, it also helps to seek advice and opinions from other people especially the Etsy community.

Moreover for the shop to stay long and you won't feel burn-out, be sure that what you are selling tickles your interest and you considered favorite. Are you fond of looking for vintage clocks or desks? Do you have the skills in using Photoshop? Do you love creating invitations? As long as you are fond of what you are doing, you are sure to stay long in Etsy and succeed in selling.

If you are not generating large sales in your first months as Etsy seller, that's fine. Stay patience and work hard to enhance your skills. Apply all the other tips incorporated in this book as well.

A Cohesive Shop

Come-up with a great assortment of items that complement each other. Think of the items in retail store, they usually sell products together there such as fashion items, baby items and home goods. However, you can also sell various items that have no connection with each other but be sure to find out how to bind your items and sell them together.

Every listing of your shop also serves as an advertisement of all the other items. Once a buyer found your shop, they already have access to other items listed. If you are selling fashion jewelleries, would a customer also consider getting other fashion accessories you offer? If someone has ordered baby clothes, she will most likely to look for other baby stuffs.

Making your shop cohesive can also attract buyers and would definitely remember your shop. For an instance, if you are selling a particular necklace and that necklace is surrounded by other jewellery with the same style and in different colors, a buyer would mostly check you shop the next time she'll look for the same items.

Don't worry as this technique won't actually limit one's creativity rather, this will help you to come up with a unique style and sense of ownership. Similarly customers can come back for other related items especially if you are selling clothes, printable items or crafting supplies.

Chapter 4

Organizing and Setting-Up

Whether you are selling vintage clothes, craft materials, offering printable templates or doing unique invitations, you should dedicate a specific space to serve as your workstation. Aside from making you more productive and efficient in you work, it also offers you the sense of ownership which can keep you motivated to work.

When creating your workspace, let your style and instincts guide you. You are maybe the type of person who loves bold colors around them or those who prefer, light and gentle surrounding to keep them focus. Remember these tips when setting your own workstation;

Area or Space - there are crafting works that require a spacious area so workers can move comfortably. Perhaps you have a spare room huge enough to accommodate your supplies, tools and other craft essentials.

The location of your workstation is also important. You may need an area with a window or you want to work quietly so you are considering taking the basement or attic. These factors can aid you to stay determined and creative while working.

Organization - crafting supplies can be a messed especially if they don't have their dedicated cabinets thus; investing in small organizers and drawers is highly advisable. It will also prevent you from losing materials and necessary tools and keeping your list of running-out stocks updated.

Keep your supplies according to its uses; ribbons, buttons, paste and glues, sewing materials, fabrics etc.

Be creative - you don't actually have to buy new drawers and cabinets. Repurposing old boxes and furniture can serve as functional storage. Customized it according to the space you need. A coat closet could be a gift-wrapping corner while old bins can turn to tools holder.

Setting-up your Finances

Once you are done with all the cleaning, decorating and planning of your workstation, it's time to manage a more important factor for your Etsy shop. Typically e-commerce and online markets require sellers and buyers to set up their payment options.

Setup paypal – creating an account with Paypal is easy however, it normally takes you a couple of days or more to have a working account with them as you need to deposit a small amount in your bank account as part of their verification purposes. It is ideal to have a separate bank account designated for your Etsy shop and have it linked with paypal.

Budgeting – part of your finances is your budget costs. Start with one month budget allotted for your supplies. Track your costing using a spreadsheet and determine if you are allotting just enough or you need to adjust. Find various stores and record their prices for the same items you are looking and from there determine where you can save.

Taxes – you can properly setup your tax information with Etsy through their website. They offer groups that will help you with this.

Setting the Etsy Account

On the contrary, setting up an account with Etsy is not that tedious. You can get a handful of information, tips and guides on the site while setting-up. Everyone will start as a buyer when they access the website. Click the "Sell" tab on top of your screen so you could access the seller account. There's a walk-through in preparing your item descriptions and uploading your images to use. You can have changes later.

For the shipping process, one must know how to package their items securely and to ship it quickly. This will help you build your reputation as an Etsy seller. Shipping supplies such as packaging tapes and bubble wraps are essential. Moreover, you must determine the average UPS shipping cost depending on the ZIP code to arrive at the right shipping charges.

Setting-up the Shipping Policies and Profiles

Read other articles that comprehensively discuss shipping options especially for international orders if you aim to go for it. You can also found related blogs with how-to articles regarding packaging. Moreover, be to fill-up shop policies and profile. The policies determine the rules for your shop and can also help buyers with their queries.

Furthermore, your profile page says everything about you and Etsy shoppers like it to be artistic. Fill this section with your crafts, your interest and related works to promote your products. Aside from attracting buyers, it will also aid you in establishing your shop specifically if you still lack feedback.

Other Tips in Setting-Up

- Use the Web Analytics in Etsy to set up the stats of your shop. Likewise you may want to set up Site Search to find out what search terms buyers are using when looking for your items.

- Enter the items in Google Base. This will make your products appear in Google Shopping results.

- Optimize your shop for Google for a better exposure.

- For more useful tips and hacks, go to Etsy Hacks. This is a site which offers time-saving tools that provide sellers special functions for their Etsy shop.

If you want your items to get feature in some places around Etsy such as its homepage, the Treasuries, Etsy Find Emails, The Storque (Etsy's blog site) and Gift Guides, make sure to use awesome photos in your items. Use appropriate tags as well and be active in the Etsy community. Moreover Etsy has its merchandising articles where you can learn about holidays to be promoted and other upcoming themes. This can aid you in your tagging of listings or to remind you that there are upcoming events where you could create and sell related items. Being feature on Gift Guides can help you increase the quantity of your item listing.

Chapter 5

Photography Musts

Perhaps you know by now that most online markets are image-driven thus, item photography is one of the essential aspects in selling and promoting your shop. Etsy allows sellers to post at least 5 images per item. Here are other tips on how to get an awesome photo to post in your online shop.

Proper lighting – we opt natural lighting, either early morning or early evening light. Direct sunlight and mid-day lighting should be avoided since these could have a negative effect on the quality of your photo and to your items as well. Avoid using the flash feature if you find the lighting still dark. Instead, increase the balance of EV on your camera as it increases the photo's "whiteness".

Select the right background – instead of using plain white backgrounds, shoot against a color or background which highlights your item. Colors can set the mood you would want to exhibit in the picture so decide which colors will complement each other. To achieve sophisticated looks, se shades of brown and purple. If the product is beige or pale brown in color, choose dark brown background. You can also be playful with colors and choose the opposite colors in the color wheel but be sure that your item will stand out.

Modern items look great with pastel and neutral colors while vintage items could be awesome with nudes and browns. **Smaller items** such as earrings must be shot with plain backgrounds so customers can focus more on the item's details. You could use some props like tabletops, old books or soft fabrics available in the house.

Larger items are great to shoot with good locations. You can get inspirations inside and outside your house. Take advantage of natural settings, architectural designs, walls with interesting details, an abandoned building or even your backyard could set the mood for your item.

How to use Photos - there are items which are better to post with a "how-to-use-it" photo. This will help your potential buyers figure out how actually the product or item is being used. It also gives them an estimate on the item's size and envisions how they can use it on a daily basis.

Close ups or Macro Mode – this is perfect in shooting smaller items like jewelries. It provides sharp outline exhibiting the details of the product.

The close-up shot will help you show-off the texture, smallest details and quality of the items to attract buyers. Invest in macro lens if you are already established with Etsy selling so you could always have a perfect shot of your items. Macro lens could be attached to your smartphone which means handiness on your part. No need to have DSLR to acquire awesome images.

Use a Model- using a model especially for clothing and jewelry items is a good idea to show the look of it when wear. They also get to know the size, length and overall look of the item by looking at the model. Moreover, you can help shoppers who are torn with sizes especially for clothe items. For non-wearable objects, you can simply stage it with its use such as a purse with card compartments and card peeking out on it.

The right angles - make the images more dynamic by taking pictures of it in various distance and angles. Some tend to post item photos which are similar with one another. Create interesting shots or search the internet on how to take awesome pictures of products using different angles.

Cropping- cropping your photo accordingly can provide it an interesting movement. It can also make your item appear closer and have the details shot. However be sure not to crap your items too tight and make the item seems cut-off and squashed.

Etsy is also popular with printable kits you can use for party items, house decorations, school labels and the like. You can take a photo of how to use it or showing its purpose so buyers can see how it will look once printed. Find the cutest spot in the house to set as background and to add elements on your image.

Grouping- is another helpful technique in taking photos of items. Arrange small items like purses, key chains, soaps and hair bows in a group shot. It will give the photo a rich look.

Additional Descriptions

Apparently, customers cannot try, touch or smell your items hence; you must be able to show them all the things they have to know in photos. To show them the size of an item, you can have that particular item shot against another object that others know the size of. Money peeping out on a purse, old books next to vintage drawer wallpaper pasted on a room are great ideas.

Macro shots can give them the "feel" of a certain item since it can capture smallest details and actual texture. For items with scents such as soaps or perfumes, place a chamomile leaves next to your chamomile perfume or some blueberries next to your soap. This will not only add attraction to your photos but can also help you in relaying product messages.

Furthermore, your descriptions can give buyers great ideas on what they might see in the additional photos.

One must not need to be a professional in photography to come-up with awesome item photos. By applying the basic techniques and tips here, you can have an interesting photo that you could use. Moreover there are free online editing software that can help you in doing some touching-up if needed. Fortunately those who are knowledgeable in Photoshop can have really great item photos using the software's various editing tools. There are also various photos editing software that does not require high level of photography skills and even a newbie can do. But be sure that you will only use these picture editors for minor editing and not for altering the entire image.

Nonetheless, setting up an online shop to success requires hard work and various steps. The tips included in the book will teach you how to take advantages of every step.

Chapter 6

More Tips that Successful Sellers Know

Here are other random tips and advice that you can also notice once you conducted your research about Etsy and how successful sellers do it.

Think as if you are the buyer - when you list a certain item, imagine you are the prospective customer. Hence you are only relying on the images and item descriptions posted on the site to get information about the product. Do you see your item a personalize one that can be used by anyone? Is it for occasional or daily use? What are the keyword you are going to use if ever you will search that same item? These information should be included in your overall list.

Spread your items - according to successful sellers on Etsy, listing your items all at once is not advisable. What they recommend is for you to list some items on a certain day then list new items on the next days. By doing such your new items will be on higher searches on Etsy which will give your shop more visibility to buyers for a longer time.

Coordinate with the Etsy Team - one good features of Etsy is their teams or the group of sellers who stay connected by a common forum or thread. It could be those who are selling same products, or the group of stay at home moms or those who are interested with crafting and do-it-yourself projects. You can learn so much from other sellers and have a sense of community. Moreover these teams provide support and motivation which can help you in running your shop.

Customer service -another important thing, providing an efficient customer service is very crucial in any kind of business. This is especially true for online shops. Treat all your buyers respectively and answer their queries as prompt as possible. Be direct about shipping charges, delivery time, policies on refund and exchanges, the modes of payment acceptable and the duty fees.

Keeping a customer waiting for almost 24 hours will most likely have them looking for other shops who can accommodate them.

Practice patience - beginners tend to get so excited with their new business however, one must be patient in doing things and would want to consider taking baby steps. Keep on enhancing your shop's profile and making better changes in selling items. These are endless tasks that successful Etsy sellers are continuously doing. Likewise there will be times that your sales is declining but keep the positivity and be more creative with your work.

Use social media - fortunately we have a myriad of ways to promote our businesses nowadays. Social media platforms are efficient tools in advertising products and services. However there are plenty of platforms which can overwhelm you thus, you have to choose one platform that you can personally check and manage. A single platform will make your task easier and customers know when and how to communicate with you. Responding on their every comment and questions is also more manageable if you only have one platform.

Set specific, attainable goals - for all of these things to transpire, a plan and a goal is a must. If your sole plan in joining Etsy is to have more money, you are most likely to fail. There are various aspects of the business that you need to plan and to have focused with. Set your financial goals first and how you can track them. A weekly goal is ideal to frequently check your sales.

Take suggestions - the best suggestions could come from your customers so take them seriously. Whilst you know what you are doing and you take time in creating and selling your items, feel free as well to take comments from customers. They could be great collaborators to make better output in the future. Don't let pride hinder you from doing this.

Moreover, you can take suggestions from other Etsy sellers. Join forums and share your experience. Don't hesitate to ask them questions and seek help with the Etsy team if there are areas you want to clarify or if you want advice to increase you sales.

Things to Avoid

Here are some of the things that you must avoid as a seller or it can affect your relationship with your customers or can have a negative impact on your sales.

Lack of communication - communication is the key. Once a buyer placed an order, it doesn't end there. You must keep on sending the messages and give them updates if necessary. You have to make a confirmation about their orders and send them ETA details.

Keep in mind that anyone who is buying in Etsy and in any other online markets is making a conscientious purchasing decision. Customers are supporting you by buying your products, complementing your handmade designs and crafts and choosing your items out of thousands and thousands of other similar products out there. Hence you need to make the feel special and well treated to encourage repeat transactions and loyalty from them.

Customers won't remember sellers only with their awesome home decors but will remember them as an individual and a great shop where they can actually communicate and place an order.

Slow turnaround of orders - if you are working with custom orders such as invitations, party favors, printable kits and the likes, you surely don't have the luxury of completing orders immediately. Let your customers know ahead of time by indicating in your list the approximate time of sending them their orders.

Whilst you consider yourself a crafter who normally takes time in creating items, consider the waiting time of your buyers as well. Let them know at the onset the possible time of delivery so they know it will take you that long.

Not checking the items - before your send those items abruptly, take time in checking them- the condition, the appearance, overall packaging, does it have the necessary parts or details and your business card. This will show that you are very keen to details and really take care of your customers.

Regardless if you send the items on-time if the items are incomplete or lacks parts, it will still earn you a negative feedback.

Acquire Exposure by Doing These

Proper categorizing- putting your items in categories appropriately will get you more exposure. To gain maximum exposure, put items that will fit in more than one category. Choose related tags in the Category Browser to find out its subcategories.

Moreover add important info to describe your item with the related tags.

Proper tags - tags serve as search terms that will help buyers to see your items. Put the necessary tags so your products will be in front of the customers. As much as possible avoid lengthy tags.

Always update your list - Etsy's default search is in reverse chronological order, hence listing regularly will ensure that your items are always on top. For several items, space your listing a bit.

Renewing - this refers to reactivating an expired listing. When you do not have an item to list on a certain day, renew an expired item. This will move the item in the higher spot of the Category Browser. However be sure that this method works fine with you in gaining exposure.

Get Advertised - Etsy has an advertising program called Showcase. Every category has its own Showcases while the Main showcase is linked with Etsy's homepage. Before purchasing a Showcase spot, make sure that you are already familiar with renewing technique and you have execute the tips and advice here to gain maximum benefit.

Again, all these will work if you are complying with the previous lessons we have discussed; good images of your items, proper listings, right keywords and tags used in listings and a neat page of you shop. These tips will make your promotions effort all worth it.

Conclusion

Thank you again for downloading this book!

I hope this book was able to help you to fully understand how Etsy works and what you need to acquire to start your journey as an Etsy seller.

The next step upon successful completion of this book is to plan for the setting up of your online shop in Etsy by completing the questions and considering the factors mentioned above. Etsy has more than a million shops thus plenty of sellers are making a living with their vintage items, handmade goods and other craft supplies. No wonder more and more people are considering to put-up an Etsy online shop.

However one must have the attitude and knowledge before they start with Etsy. This maybe a viable business venture but not for those who are lacks the information and selling skills. This book will serve as your guide on learning the work-around in Etsy. After this, continue reading and searching to expand your knowledge with Etsy selling.

Finally, if you enjoyed this book, please take the time to share your thoughts and post a review on Amazon. It'd be greatly appreciated!

Thank you and good luck!

Made in the USA
Coppell, TX
07 March 2021